T0128611

ANIMALS IN THE BIBLE

A Book of Lessons from God's Creations

Written and Illustrated by LYNN CALOS ARCE

WestBow Press books may be ordered through booksellers or by contacting:

WestBow Press
A Division of Thomas Nelson & Zondervan
1663 Liberty Drive
Bloomington, IN 47403
www.westbowpress.com
1 (866) 928-1240

Because of the dynamic nature of the Internet, any web addresses or links contained in this book may have changed since publication and may no longer be valid. The views expressed in this work are solely those of the author and do not necessarily reflect the views of the publisher, and the publisher hereby disclaims any responsibility for them.

Any people depicted in stock imagery provided by Getty Images are models, and such images are being used for illustrative purposes only.
Certain stock imagery © Getty Images.

Interior Image Credit: Lynn Calos Arce

Scripture quotations marked NIV are taken from The Holy Bible, New International Version®, NIV® Copyright © 1973, 1978, 1984, 2011 by Biblica, Inc.® Used by permission. All rights reserved worldwide.

Scripture quotations marked NIRV taken from the Holy Bible, New International Reader's Version®. Copyright © 1996, 1998 Biblica. All rights reserved throughout the world. Used by permission of Biblica.

ISBN: 978-1-9736-9424-3 (sc)
ISBN: 978-1-9736-9423-6 (hc)
ISBN: 978-1-9736-9425-0 (e)

Library of Congress Control Number: 2020911152

Print information available on the last page.

WestBow Press rev. date: 08/31/2020

WestBow
PRESS®
A DIVISION OF THOMAS NELSON
& ZONDERVAN

For those who delight with God's amazing creations.

May the animals' roars, moos, baas, and tweets

be a constant reminder of God's love and majestic design.

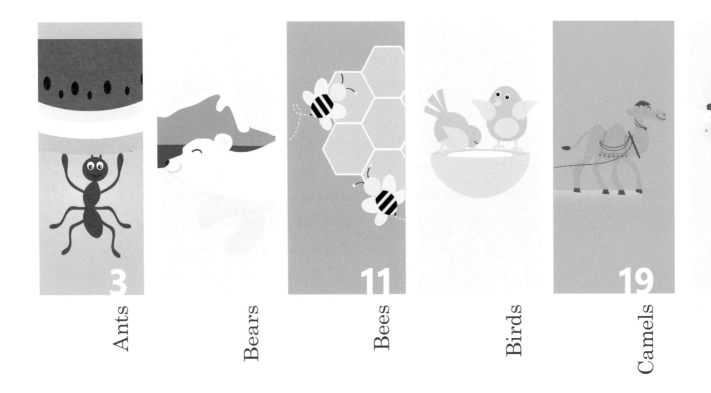

WHAT'S INSIDE....

Featured Animals in the Bible

Cows

Fish

Lions **31**

Owls **35**

Roosters **39**

Sheep **43**

"...for the world is mine, and all that is in it."
Psalms 50:12 NIV

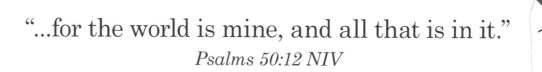

God made everything!

God has always been there. He made everything from stars, moons, heavens, and even the small creatures that crawl on the earth.

"For since the creation of the world God's invisible qualities—his eternal power and divine nature—have been clearly seen, being understood from what has been made, so that people are without excuse."
Romans 1:20 NIV

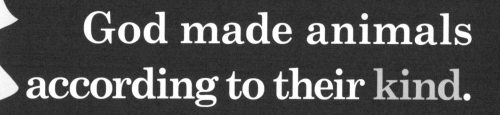

God made animals according to their kind.

The Bible tells us that God made each animal after its kind. He designed things to work a certain way. When giraffes make baby giraffes, you get giraffes and not zebras; so there is a giraffe kind. It works the same with sheep, dogs, chickens, and other animals.

"God made the wild animals according to their kinds,
the livestock according to their kinds,
and all the creatures that move along the ground
according to their kinds.
And God saw that it was good."
Genesis 1:25 NIV

Ants

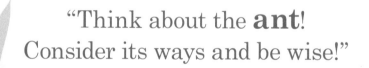

"Think about the **ant**!
Consider its ways and be wise!"

Proverbs 6:6 NIRV

What Can We Learn?

Do you sometimes feel like you don't want to do homework or household chores? The Bible warns us of the danger of laziness and directs us to the ants because their ways are wise (Proverbs 6:6-8, 11 NIRV). They teach us the value of hard work, how to prepare for the future, and how to be self-motivated. So the next time we see some crawling ants, let them be a reminder that we can be diligent, too!

My Prayer

The ants are smart. The ants are wise.
Teach me their ways, so I will not be unwise.

FUN FACTS

Adult Female: Queen
Adult Male: Drones
Group of Ants: Colony
Young Ant: Larva

Some ants can swim.
Some ants have no eyes.
Ants have two stomachs,
one to hold food for themselves
and another to hold food to
share with others.

"Four things on earth that are small. But they are very wise: Ants are creatures of little strength, yet they store up their food in the summer."
Proverbs 30:24-25 NIRV

Bears

"It is better to meet a **bear** whose cubs have been stolen than to meet a foolish person who is acting foolishly."

Proverbs 17:12 NIRV

What Can We Learn?

Bears are strong and mighty. Mama bears are known to protect their cubs from danger. God is like that, too! He protects us from danger. The Bible said, *"The Lord will keep you from all harm. He will watch over your life."*

(Psalms 121:7 NIV)

My Prayer

Lord, please keep me in your watch wherever I go. Embrace me with your love as I grow and grow.

Bees

"They swarmed around me like **bees**..."

Psalms 118:12 NIRV

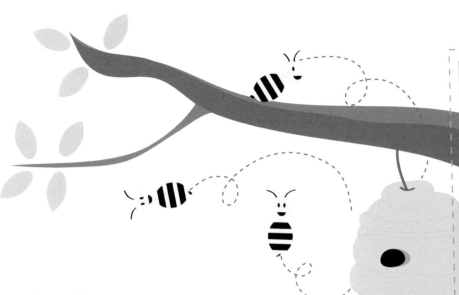

What Can We Learn?

Did you know that each bee has a different role in the hive? God designed the bees to perform different roles in their colony. Some bees work as builders, nurses, cleaners, and many more. Just like these amazing bees, God gave us different talents, too! The Bible tells us to use our talents to work together for the Lord. *"We all have gifts. They differ according to the grace God has given to each of us."* (Romans 12:6 NIRV)

My Prayer

Lord, the talents that you gave us are not all the same.
Teach me to use them to glorify your name.

FUN FACTS

Female Bee: Workers
Male Bee: Drones
Group of Bees: Swarm or Colony
Young Bee: Larvae

Bees may need to fly 50,000 miles to make 1 pound of honey. It is like going around the world twice. Wow, that's a lot of flying!

Birds

And God said, "Let the water teem with living creatures, and let **birds** fly above the earth across the vault of the sky."
Genesis 1:20 NIV

17

What Can We Learn?

The Bible tells us that God knows every bird that He made. *"I know every bird in the mountains,"* says the Lord (Psalms 50:11 NIV). He takes care of them. In the same way, God cares for each one of us. His love for us is overflowing. If we put our trust in Him, we are surely sheltered under His wings.

"He will cover you with his feathers, and under his wings you will find refuge; his faithfulness will be your shield and rampart." (Psalms 91:4 NIV)

FUN FACTS

Adult Female: Hen
Adult Male: Male
Group of Birds: Flock or Flight
Young Bird: Chick

Birds do not have teeth.
They have bills.
If an animal has feathers,
it is a bird!

*"Look at the birds of the air...
But your Father who is
in heaven feeds them.
Aren't you worth
much more than they are?"*
Matthew 6:26 NIV

My Prayer

Lord, thank you for all the birds in the air.
They remind me of your unconditional love and care.

Camels

"Again I tell you, it is easier for a **camel**
to go through the eye of a needle than
for someone who is rich to enter the kingdom of God."

Matthew 19:24 NIV

Lemons

Tomatoes

Cucumber

What Can We Learn?

Camels are large animals. Entering an extremely tiny space may be a challenge for them. When Jesus said that *it is easier for a camel to go through the eye of a needle than for someone who is rich to enter the kingdom of God* (Matthew 19:24 NIV), He gave us a clear picture of what difficult or impossible means. Rejoice! Nothing is too difficult for Him to do. Jesus declared, *"What is impossible with man is possible with God,"* (Luke 18:27 NIV). So when life presents us with a difficult task, keep in mind what Jesus had said, *"You may ask me anything in my name, and I will do it."* (John 14:14 NIV)

FUN FACTS

Adult Female: Cow
Adult Male: Bull
Group of Camel: Flock
Young Camel: Calf

Camels have long eyelashes and hair in their ears to protect themselves from blowing sand. They have bony arches over their eyes, which they use as a sun shield. Wow, God made a pair of built-in sunglasses to protect their eyes!

My Prayer

Nothing is impossible with you, O Lord.
Help me understand and trust in your word.

Cows

"The **cow** will feed with the bear..."
Isaiah 11:7 NIV

What Can We Learn?

Did you know that Jacob, son of Isaac, used cows as a peace offering to his brother, Esau? The Bible tells us to say sorry when we do something wrong to our parents, friends, and especially to God. However, we do not need to offer a cow to help heal our relationship with God. Jesus did it already by dying on the cross. *"God gave Christ as a sacrifice to pay for sins through the spilling of his blood. So God forgives the sins of those who have faith."* (Romans 3:25 NIRV)

FUN FACTS

Adult Female: Cow
Adult Male: Bull
Group of Cow: Herd
Young Cow: Calf

You can check how old a cow is by counting the rings on its horn. A cow can drink up to 25-50 gallons of water. That's about a bathtub full!

My Prayer

Jesus, you died for our sake.
Come in to my life, O Lord.
You have my whole heart to take.

Fish

"From inside the **fish** Jonah prayed to the LORD his God. He said: "In my distress I called to the LORD, and he answered me. From deep in the realm of the dead I called for help, and you listened to my cry."

Jonah 2:1-2 NIV

WORLD'S
BIGGEST FISH

WHALE SHARK
40 Feet

What Can We Learn?

In the story of Jonah and the big fish, God used the big fish to swallow Jonah when he was trying to escape from what God had wanted him to do. *"Jonah ran away from the Lord,"* (Jonah 1:3 NIV). We sometimes desire to flee than to follow God. When God wants something to happen, there is no way we can escape from it. He knows what is best for us. The Bible said, *"For I know the plans I have for you," declares the Lord, "plans to prosper you and not to harm you, plans to give you hope and a future."* (Jeremiah 29:11 NIV)

My Prayer

You are abounding in love and forgiving, too.
I'm sorry, Father God, if I flee from you.
Clean my heart, O Lord, so I can truly follow you.

FUN FACTS

Adult Female: Fish
Adult Male: Fish
Group of Fish: School
Young Fish: Fry

Whale Sharks are the biggest fish in the ocean. Some fish swim together to survive or evade hungry predators. Although jellyfish and crayfish have the word "fish" in their name, they are not fish.

I'm not a fish!

Lions

"The wicked flee though no one pursues,
but the righteous are as bold as a **lion**."

Proverbs 28:1 NIV

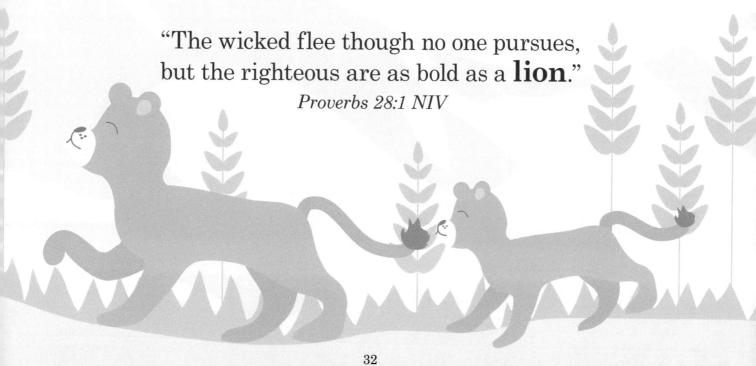

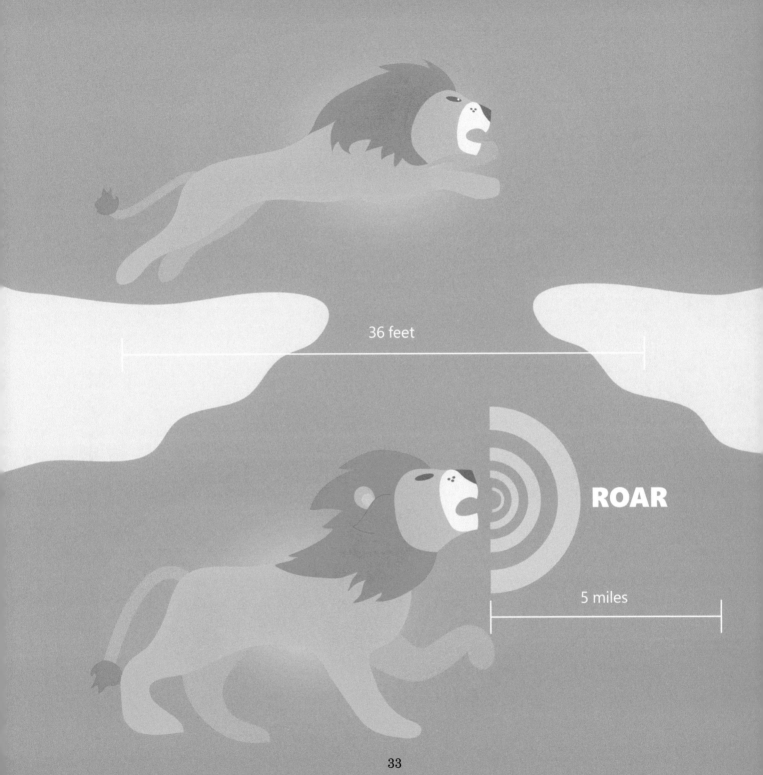

36 feet

ROAR

5 miles

What Can We Learn?

"The first is a lion, which is mighty among the animals. It doesn't back away from anything." (Proverbs 30:30 NIRV)

Lions are majestic species that possess great power and strength. They can leap up to 36 feet, and they can loudly roar—can be heard as far as 5 miles. Even though lions can do mighty things, God is stronger and more powerful than anything in this world. He revealed His power to us in many ways throughout the Bible: He shut the mouths of the lions (Daniel 6:22 NIV), He created the world (Isaiah 45:12 NIV), and He formed every human heart (Psalms 33:15 NIV). Our God is truly amazing! Surely, there is no limit to what He can do.

My Prayer

Lord, you have done so many great things for us. Our hearts are full of love, and we are filled with joy.

FUN FACTS

Female Lion: Lioness
Male Lion: Lion
Group of Lions: Pride
Young Lion: Cub

Lions belong to the Felidae family, which includes cats, tigers, leopards, panthers, lynxes, pumas, and cheetahs. Lions love to live together with their group or pride. Although they are known as the "king of the jungle," they do not live in the jungle. Their real habitats are in the grasslands and plains where they can openly hunt for food.

KING OF THE PLAINS

Owls

"The little **owl**, the cormorant, the great owl, the white owl, the desert owl, the osprey."
Leviticus 11:17-18 NIV

37

What Can We Learn?

Most owls are nocturnal birds, which means they are active and normally hunt for food at night. The Bible tells us that God provides everything we need. He is awake in the morning and at night time, too! *"My help comes from the Lord, the Maker of heaven and earth. He will not let your foot slip—he who watches over you will not slumber."* (Psalms 121:2-3 NIV)

My Prayer

Thank you God for the owls at night.

I know that I never leave your sight, especially at night.

FUN FACTS

Adult Female: Female Owl
Adult Male: Male Owl
Group of Owls: Parliament
Young Owl: Owlet

Owls have excellent eyesight at night. Because they can't move their eyes, they stretch their necks to turn their heads 270 degrees! They do not make their nests. They nest in a woodpecker hole or in a hollow tree.

270 degrees

Roosters

Then Peter remembered the word Jesus had spoken:
"Before the **rooster** crows,
you will disown me three times."
And he went outside and wept bitterly.
Matthew 26:75 NIV

What Can We Learn?

Have you heard the rooster crow in the morning? What does it remind you of? The rooster's crows each morning remind us that a new day has come. In some places, people use this sound like a daily reminder that they should get ready. What a great alarm clock! The Bible tells us many times that we should always be watchful and ready for the second coming of our Lord Jesus Christ (Mark 13:32, 35-36 NIV). We should not wait for the rooster to announce the morning for our hearts to be ready. We should, therefore, be alert at all times.

My Prayer

Dear God, you know where I am going and what I am doing.
Guide me always for I know your love is enduring.

FUN FACTS

Adult Female: Hen
Adult Male: Rooster
Group: Brood
Young Male: Cockerel
Young Female: Pullet
Newly Hatched: Chick

Roosters are chicken, and they belong to the bird kind. They do not have teeth. They swallow their food whole and use their stomach to grind their food up. They can dance, too! Their dance is called tidbitting, which requires the roosters to make a 'took took' sound as they move their head up and down. It signals other chickens that yummy food is available.

We are family!

Sheep

"We all, like **sheep**, have gone astray, each of us has turned to our own way."

Isaiah 53:6 NIV

What Can We Learn?

Sheep recognize the voice of their shepherd. It brings them comfort and security. They are totally dependent upon their shepherd as they graze. Their shepherd's watchful eyes keep them away from danger. Did you know that Jesus is our Shepherd? He is the True Shepherd, who gives His life and offers the doorway to access heaven, for *He is the way, the truth, and the life* (John 10:9-11, 14:6 NIV). Jesus also said, *"My sheep listen to my voice; I know them, and they follow me."* (John 10:27 NIV)

FUN FACTS

Adult Female: Ewe
Adult Male: Ram
Group of Sheep: Herd or Flock
Young Sheep: Lamb

Sheep get lost easily. They can quickly wander away from the flock while they graze.

My Prayer

Sorry, Lord, if I sometimes wander away. Show me the way, so I will be ok.

"But ask the animals, and they will teach you,

or the birds in the sky, and they will tell you;

or speak to the earth, and it will teach you,

or let the fish in the sea inform you.

Which of all these does not know

that the hand of the Lord has done this?

In his hand is the life of every creature

and the breath of all mankind."

Job 12:7-10 NIV